THE LIBRARY OF CONSTELLATIONS™

Andromeda

Stephanie True Peters

The Rosen Publishing Group's

PowerKids Press™

New York

For Chloe, my little princess

Published in 2003 by The Rosen Publishing Group, Inc.
29 East 21st Street, New York, NY 10010

First Edition

Editors: Veronica Vergoth, Natashya Wilson
Book Design: Michael J. Caroleo, Michael Donnellan, Michael de Guzman
Photo Credits: Cover and pp. 4, 12 © John Sanford/SPL/Photo Researchers Inc., graphic enhancement by Michael Caroleo; title page and p. 8 © Bode's Uranographia, 1801, courtesy of the Science, Industry & Business Library, the New York Public Library, Astor, Lenox and Tilden Foundations; pp. 6–7 © Stapleton Collection/CORBIS; p. 11 © Kym Thalassoudis, digital manipulation by Michael de Guzman; p. 15 © Michael Nicholson/CORBIS; p. 16 © NOAO/AURA/NSF; p. 19 by Photodisc; p. 20 © Bill Schoening, Vanessa Harvey/REU program/NOAO/AURA/NSF.

Peters, Stephanie True, 1965–
Andromeda / Stephanie True Peters.— 1st ed.
    p. cm. — (The library of constellations)
Includes bibliographical references and index.
Summary: Provides historic and scientific information about the constellation Andromeda as well as about stars in general.
  ISBN 0-8239-6165-6 (library binding)
1. Andromeda (Constellation)—Juvenile literature. 2. Andromeda Galaxy—Juvenile literature. [1. Andromeda (Constellation) 2. Andromeda Galaxy.] I. Title.
  QB802 .P4 2003
  523.8—dc21
                                                                                2001004546

Manufactured in the United States of America

Contents

The Princess in the Sky

For thousands of years, people have mapped outlines of humans, animals, and objects in the stars. People who mapped these outlines gave them names. A star outline that has been named is called a constellation. One group of constellations is named for a royal family from mythology. This royal group of constellations has a king, his queen, and their daughter, the princess. The princess is named Andromeda. About 10 main stars make up her constellation. Many fainter stars are also part of Andromeda. The four brightest stars form a curved line that is easy to see on a clear night. Other stars form a second line from the same starting point. Together the two lines make a *V* shape.

Fun Facts

Eighty-eight constellations have been mapped in the sky. Of all of these constellations, Andromeda, Cassiopeia, and Virgo are the only three that represent women. The rest represent men, animals, or objects.

The point of the V represents Andromeda's head. The two lines form her body. The stars that form the bottom line in this picture are the easiest to see in the night sky.

How to Find the Princess

To find Andromeda, first find the star formation called the Big Dipper. The Big Dipper is an **asterism**, or a group of stars within another constellation. It is made of seven stars and looks like a square bowl with a bent handle. Trace a line from the two stars on the outer edge of the Big Dipper's bowl to the North Star, called **Polaris**. On the other side of Polaris, look for a group of stars that forms a *W* shape. This is the constellation **Cassiopeia**, named for Andromeda's mother. Andromeda is on the other side of Cassiopeia. The star in the point of Andromeda's *V* shape is part of another constellation, called **Pegasus**, the Flying Horse. This star is one of the four corners of the Great Square, an asterism that is part of Pegasus. You can find Andromeda by finding the Great Square.

In North America, you can see Andromeda best in the autumn and in the winter. In South America, you can see Andromeda best in the spring.

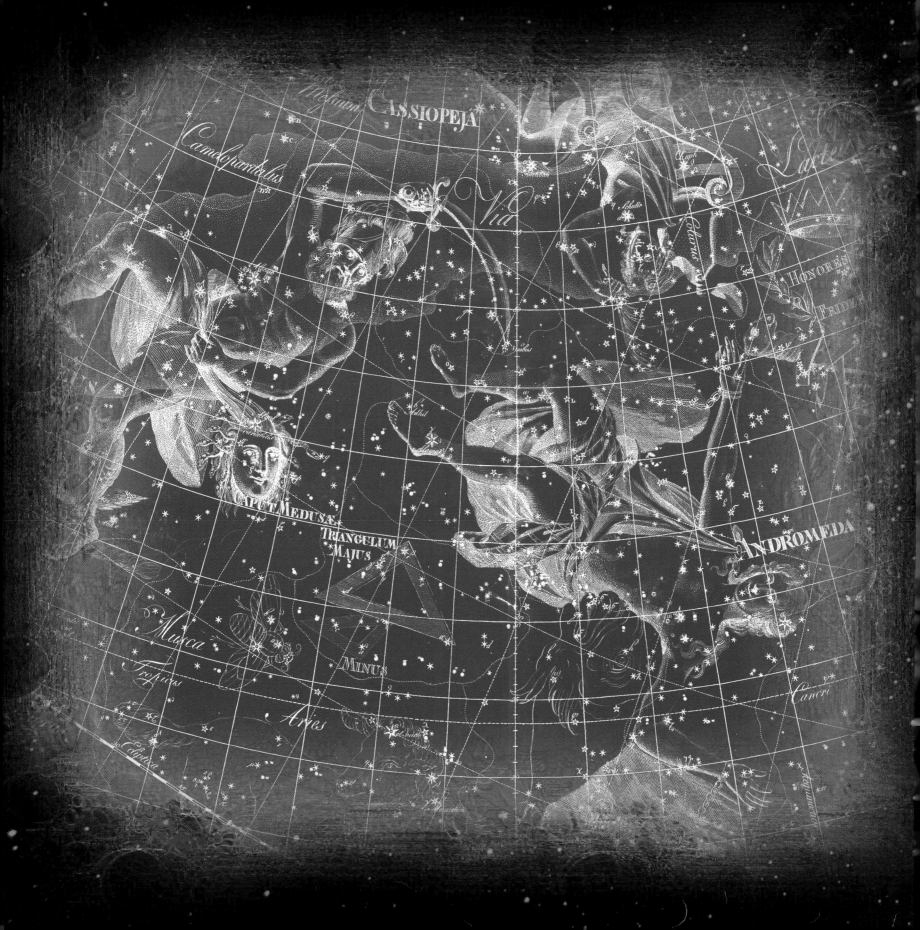

The Andromeda Myth

Many constellations are named for people and creatures from myths. The ancient Greeks, who lived around 3,000 B.C., told the myth of Andromeda. She was the daughter of King **Cepheus** and Queen Cassiopeia. Cassiopeia bragged that Andromeda was lovelier than the sea **nymphs**. This angered the sea god, **Poseidon**. Poseidon sent a dreadful sea monster to destroy King Cepheus's kingdom. The kingdom would be saved only if Andromeda were chained to a rock to be eaten by the sea monster. Just as the monster was about to attack Andromeda, **Perseus** flew by on Pegasus, the winged horse. Perseus was the son of **Zeus**, the king of the Greek gods. Perseus fell in love with Andromeda and killed the monster by cutting off its head with his sword. In a different telling of this myth, Perseus killed the monster by showing it the head of Medusa, a horrible creature with snakes for hair. The monster looked at Medusa's head and turned into stone. In both tellings, Perseus and Andromeda were married. **Athena**, the Greek goddess of wisdom, placed them together in the sky when they died.

In the night sky, the constellation Perseus rests at Andromeda's feet. Some of Perseus's stars make a curved line that is shaped like a hook.

The Perseus Family

The royal constellations of Andromeda, Cassiopeia, and Cepheus are all part of a larger group of constellations known as the Perseus Family. These constellations are near one another in the night sky. The constellations Perseus, Pegasus, Cetus, Auriga, Lacerta, and Triangulum also belong to the Perseus Family. To find the Perseus Family constellations, first find Cassiopeia's *W* shape. Andromeda is on one side of Cassiopeia. Cepheus is on the other. Perseus stands at Andromeda's feet. Auriga, the **Charioteer**, is on the other side of Perseus. Pegasus soars above Andromeda. Triangulum, the Triangle, is close to Andromeda's brightest line of stars. Lacerta, the Lizard, is between Cassiopeia and Pegasus. Cetus, the Whale, is farther away from the other constellations. It lies above Pegasus's back. Cetus also belongs to another family of constellations, the Heavenly Waters.

This illustration shows Andromeda surrounded by Triangulum, Perseus, Cassiopeia, Cepheus, Lacerta, and Pegasus. Cetus and Auriga are farther away, beyond Pegasus and Perseus.

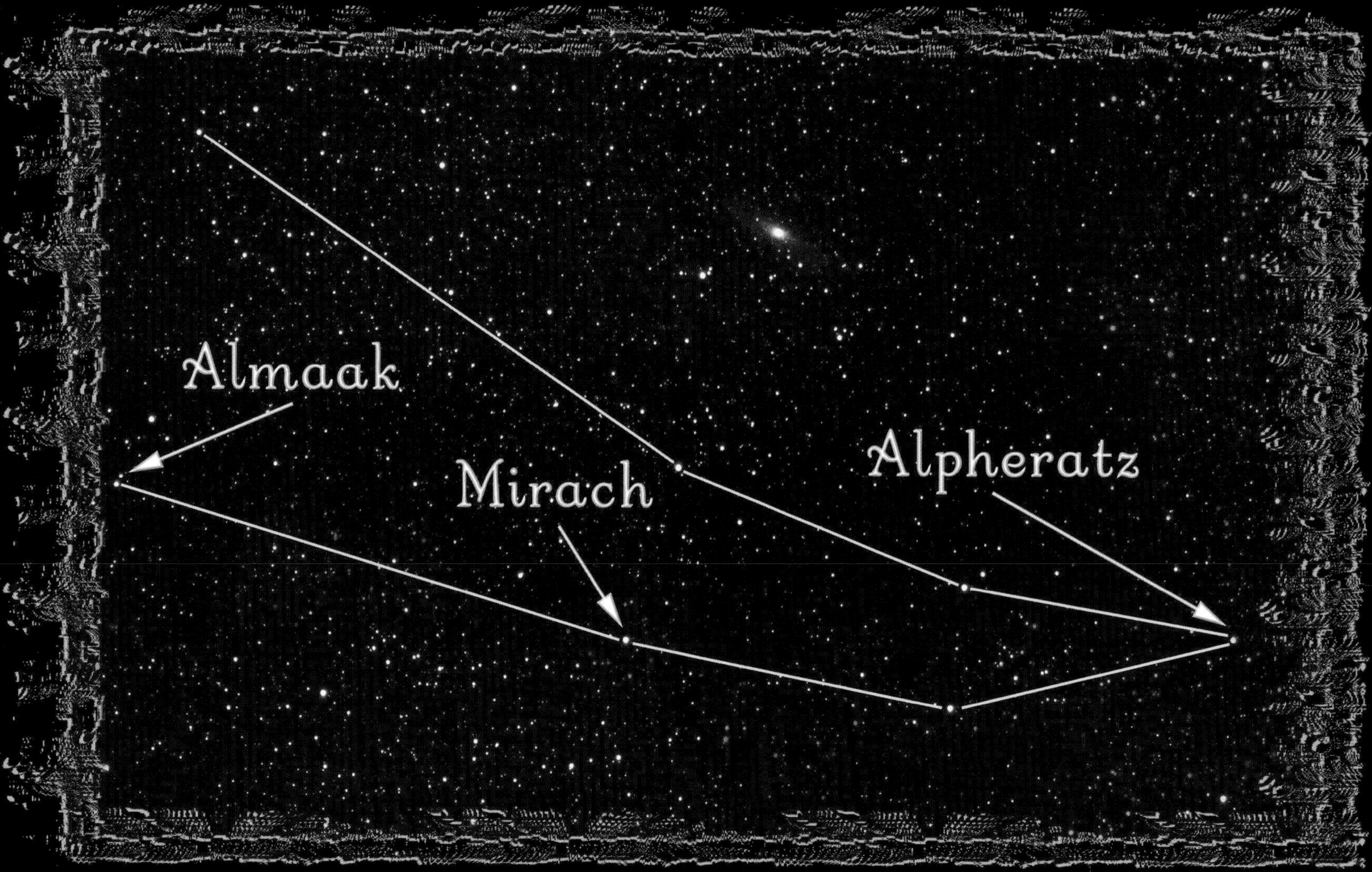
Almaak
Mirach
Alpheratz

Arab Star Names

Three of Andromeda's four brightest stars have Arab names. These star names are very old. Arab skywatchers gave the stars their names centuries ago. These ancient Arabs lived in about 300 B.C., in what today is Saudi Arabia in the Middle East. To find the three stars that the ancient Arabs named, first find the star Andromeda shares with Pegasus. This star is usually called Alpheratz, though sometimes it's called Sirrah. Alpheratz means "horse's **navel**." Follow the line of stars away from Pegasus. The next bright star doesn't have an Arab name, but the one after it does. It is called Mirach, which means "the **loins**." The last star in the line is named Almaak. Almaak is also spelled Almach. This star was named for an Arabian, weasel-like animal!

Alpheratz and Mirach are the brightest stars in Andromeda. Almaak, the next-brightest star, is actually made of four stars that circle around one another.

Star Names: Letters and Numbers

Every star in a constellation has a name. One system for naming stars was invented by German **astronomer** Johann Bayer, in 1603. Starting with the brightest star, he gave each star in a constellation a letter from the Greek alphabet. He then added a Latin spelling of the constellation name. Alpheratz is the brightest star of Andromeda, so its Bayer name is Alpha Andromedae. "Alpha" is the Greek letter *A*. The next-brightest star is named Beta Andromedae. "Beta" is the Greek letter *B*. In the early 1700s, an Englishman named John Flamsteed introduced a new naming system. Instead of letters, he used numbers with the Latin name of the constellation. Unlike letters, numbers never run out, so more stars could be named under Flamsteed's system. Stars are numbered across a constellation from west to east. Alpheratz is 21 Andromedae, because it is the twenty-first star in Andromeda if you start counting from the westernmost star in the constellation. Today many stars are still known by the letters and the numbers that Bayer and Flamsteed used.

In 1675, King Charles II made John Flamsteed England's first Astronomer Royal. Flamsteed's records of the stars were first published in 1712.

Fun Facts

At age 14, Flamsteed had health problems. His father would not let him go to school, so Flamsteed studied astronomy on his own. After becoming Astronomer Royal in 1675, Flamsteed helped to build the Royal Observatory in Greenwich, England. Flamsteed fought to keep his work from being published before it was ready. When 400 copies of his unfinished work were published in 1712, Flamsteed destroyed 300 of them! His complete work, a book of 3,000 stars, was published in 1725, more than 5 years after his death.

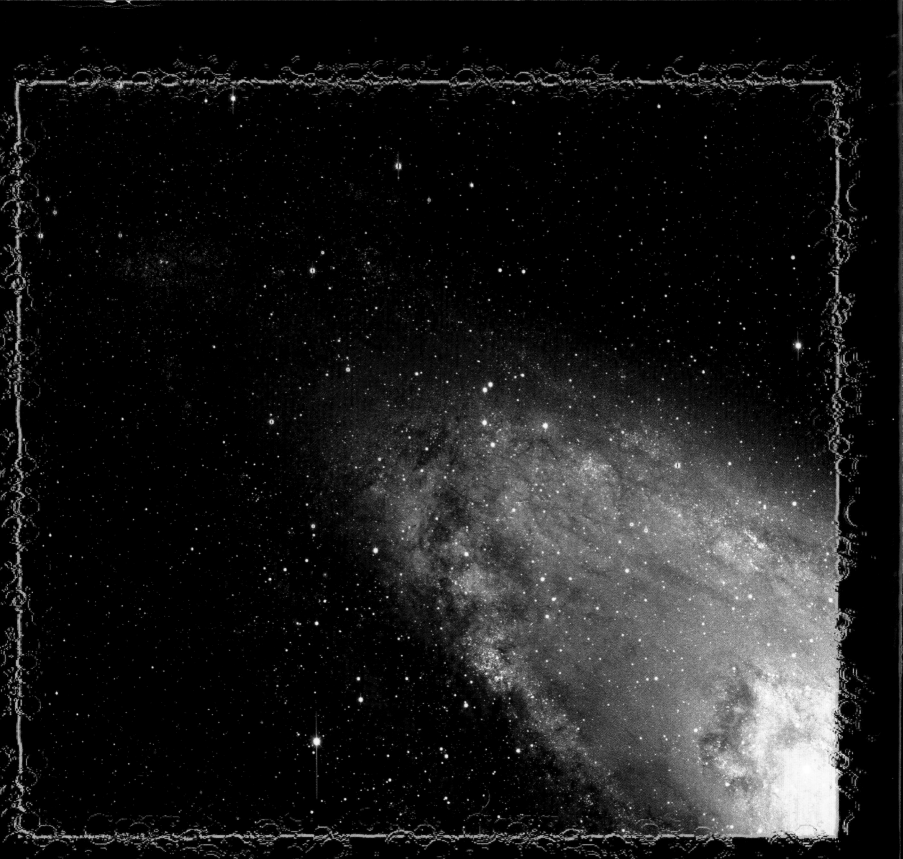

Charles Messier

Telescopes are instruments that use lenses and mirrors to magnify objects in the sky. Telescopes were invented in the 1600s. Since that time astronomers have been using telescopes to discover the secrets of the universe. In the 1700s, French astronomer Charles Messier used telescopes to search for **comets**. While searching he observed many other mysterious objects in the sky. In 1759, he began to list the objects he saw. He published a list of 103 objects in 1781. Today Messier's list has 110 objects. It includes all the objects found by Messier after his first list was published. They became known as M, or Messier, objects. Messier objects include **galaxies**, **star clusters**, and **nebulae**, which are clouds of dust and gas. One of the objects Messier numbered is found in the Andromeda constellation. It is known as M31, the Andromeda Galaxy.

If you look closely at this picture of the northwest part of M31, you'll see that stars have colors. Bluish stars are the youngest. Yellow and red stars are older.

What Is a Galaxy?

A galaxy is a huge cluster of stars, gas, and dust held together by **gravity**. There are more than 10 billion galaxies in the universe. Galaxies come in different shapes and sizes. When seen from above, a spiral galaxy looks like a pinwheel with blurry arms. From the side, it looks like a flat disk with a ball stuck through the center. A barred spiral galaxy looks like a spiral galaxy, except its center is shaped like a bar. An elliptical galaxy looks like a flattened ball. An irregular galaxy doesn't have a definite shape. Irregular galaxies are usually smaller than the other types of galaxies. The Andromeda Galaxy is a large spiral galaxy. Our **solar system** is part of another spiral galaxy, called the Milky Way.

Fun Facts

The Sun and our solar system are located on one of the arms of the Milky Way's spiral. Just as Earth circles the Sun, the Sun and all the stars in the Milky Way circle the Milky Way's center. It takes Earth one year to circle the Sun. It takes the Sun about 250 million years to circle the Milky Way's center!

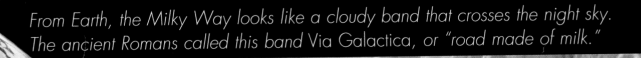

From Earth, the Milky Way looks like a cloudy band that crosses the night sky. The ancient Romans called this band Via Galactica, or "road made of milk."

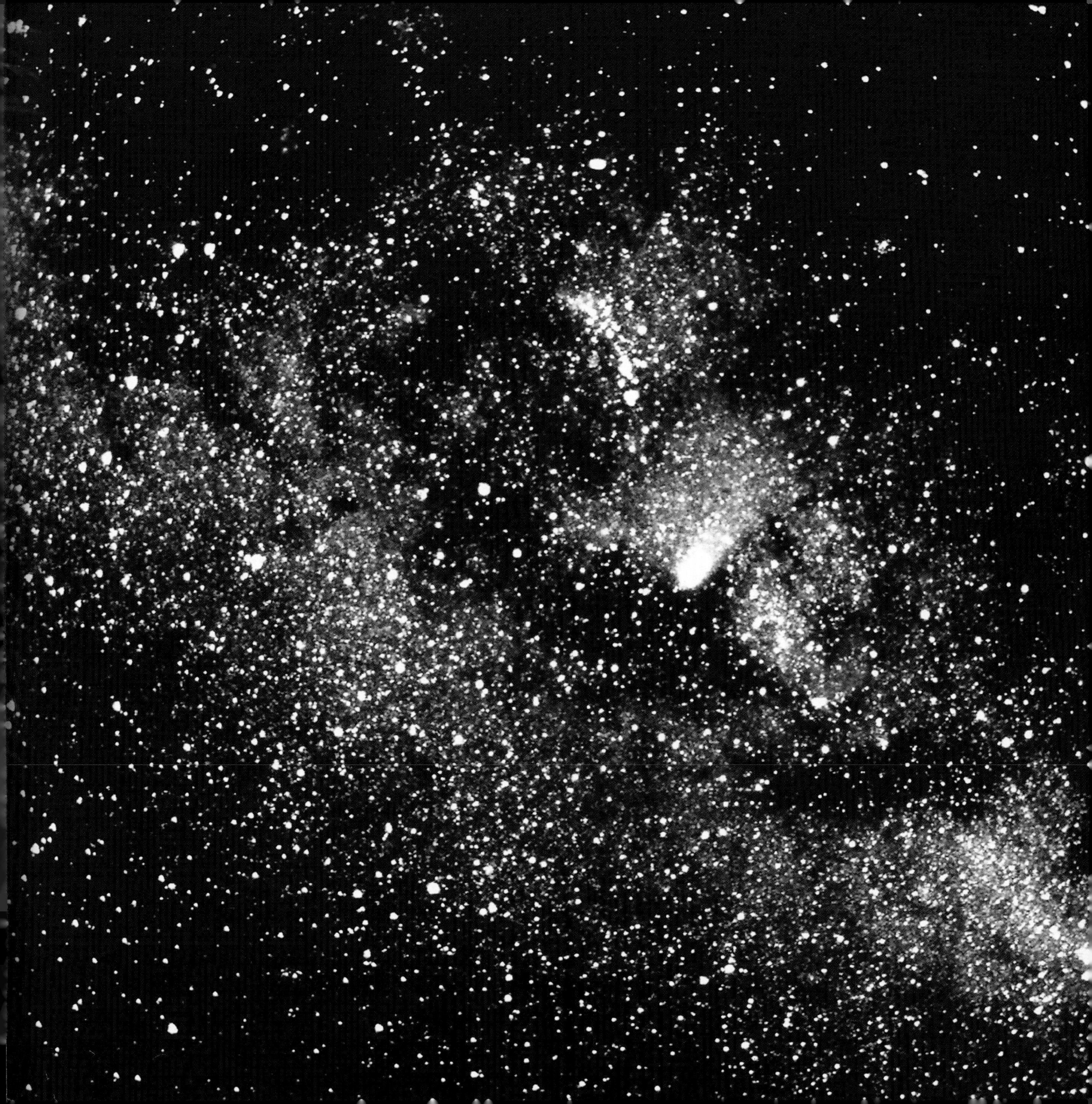

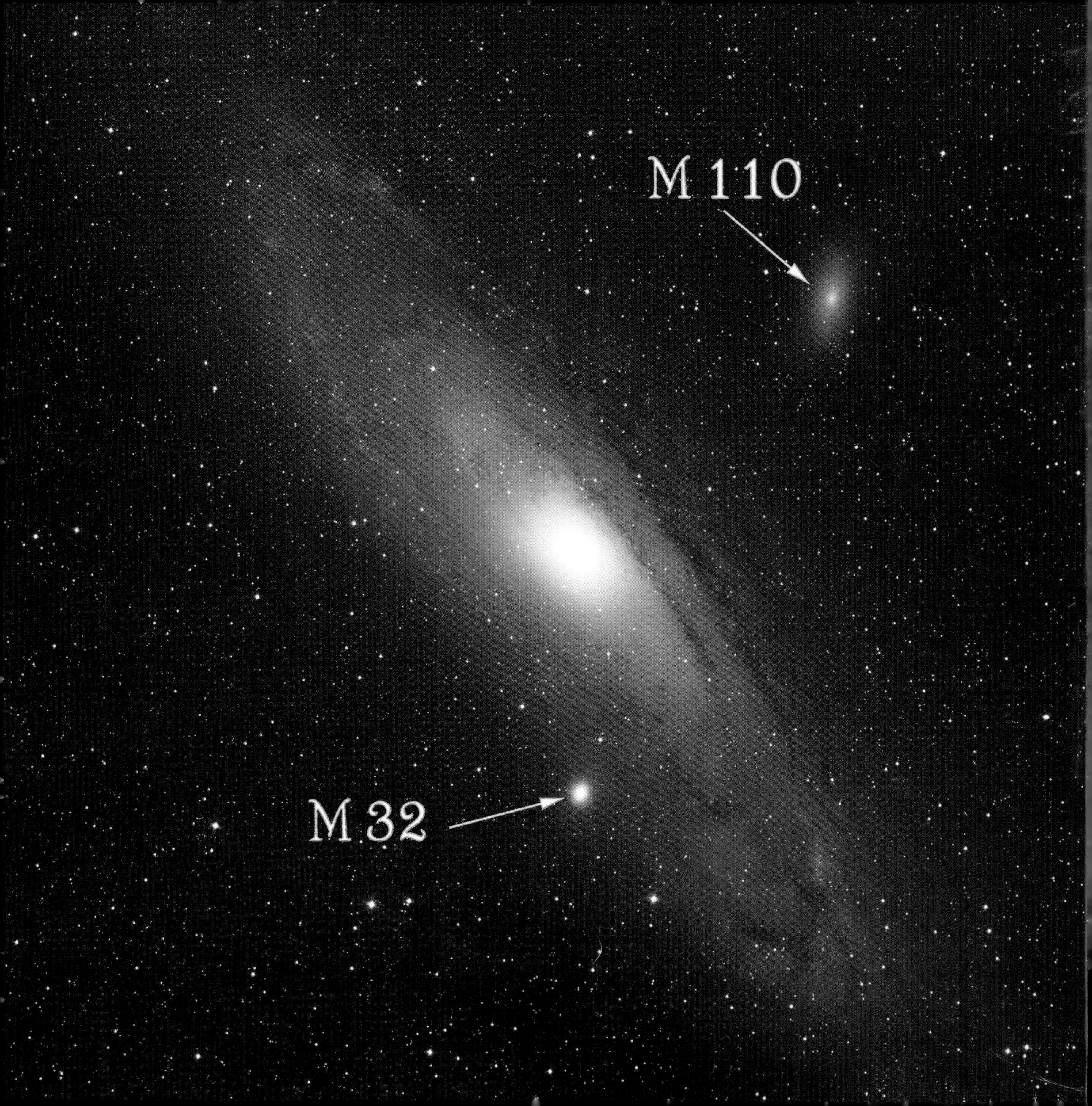
M 110
M 32

The Andromeda Galaxy

The Andromeda Galaxy, or M31, is one of the best-known spiral galaxies in the universe. It is more than 2 million **light-years** away from Earth and is the closest major galaxy to us. One light-year is the distance that light can travel through space in one year, about 6 trillion miles (10 trillion km). Two million light-years is very, very far away! M31 is also the largest known galaxy. It has about 300 billion stars. On a clear night, it is the farthest thing that can be seen with the naked eye. To find it, look for Alpheratz and Mirach. Then find Cassiopeia, the *W*-shaped constellation. M31 lies within the triangle formed by Alpheratz, Mirach, and the second point of the *W*. From Earth, M31 looks like a blurry, stretched-out spot. For many years, astronomers thought this blurry spot was a nebula, not a galaxy. When they figured out how large M31 really was, they renamed it a galaxy.

Near M31 are two more Messier objects, the elliptical galaxies M32 and M110. M32 is the spot at the edge of M31. M110 is the spot above M31.

The Local Group

The Andromeda Galaxy and the Milky Way are the most important members of the group of galaxies known as the Local Group. The Local Group includes 30 galaxies that are near to us. By studying these galaxies, astronomers can learn more about the universe and the galaxy in which we live. The Andromeda Galaxy is particularly interesting to scientists because it is similar to the Milky Way. It is difficult to have a clear idea of what our own galaxy is like because we can't look at it from the outside. The Andromeda Galaxy is easier for scientists to observe. The more we learn about the Andromeda Galaxy, the more we know about the Milky Way. Fortunately finding this important galaxy will always be easy. Simply find the constellation of the princess it's named for, and you'll find the galaxy!

Glossary

asterism (AS-tuh-rih-zem) A group of stars that is part of a constellation.

astronomer (uh-STRAH-nuh-mer) A person who studies stars, planets, and outer space.

Athena (uh-THEE-nuh) The Greek goddess of wisdom, from Greek mythology.

Cassiopeia (ka-see-uh-PEE-uh) Queen of Ethiopia, mother of Andromeda, and wife of Cepheus, from Greek mythology.

Cepheus (SEE-fyuhs) King of Ethiopia, father of Andromeda, and husband of Cassiopeia, from Greek mythology.

charioteer (cha-ree-uh-TEER) Someone who drives a chariot, which is a fancy cart pulled by horses.

comets (KAH-mits) Heavenly bodies, made of ice and dust, that look like stars with tails of light.

galaxies (GA-lik-seez) Huge clusters of stars, dust, and clouds, with spiral, spiral barred, elliptical, or irregular shapes.

gravity (GRA-vih-tee) The force that draws objects toward one another.

light-years (LYT-yeerz) The distance light can travel in one year, 6 trillion miles (10 trillion km).

loins (LOYNZ) The area of the lower stomach and the upper thighs.

navel (NAY-vul) The center of the stomach, or bellybutton.

nebulae (NEH-byuh-lee) Clouds of dust and gas, the birthplace of stars. Plural of nebula.

nymphs (NIHMFS) Beautiful maidens who live in the forests and in water, in Greek myths.

Pegasus (PEH-guh-suhs) A horse with wings, from Greek mythology.

Perseus (PER-see-us) Son of Zeus and hero of Greek mythology.

Polaris (poh-LAR-is) The North Star, or polestar.

Poseidon (poh-SY-dun) Greek god of the sea, from Greek mythology.

solar system (SOH-ler SIS-tum) A group of planets that circles a star.

star clusters (STAR KLUS-terz) Giant collections of stars drawn together by the force of gravity.

Zeus (ZOOS) King of the Greek gods and goddesses, from Greek mythology.

Index

Web Sites

To learn more about constellations and Andromeda, check out these Web sites:
www.enchantedlearning.com
www.hubblesite.org
    www.lhs.berkeley.edu/starclock